T0368423

METUSELA ALBERT

GOD DID NOT HAVE A BEGOTTEN SON.

(John and Paul Contradicted Genesis 1:1 & Isaiah 43:10-11).

To order additional copies of this book, contact:

Xlibris
844-714-8691
www.Xlibris.com
Orders@Xlibris.com

ISBN: Softcover   979-8-3694-2944-0
       EBook   979-8-3694-2943-3

Print information available on the last page

Rev. date: 09/06/2024

Contents

SCRIPTURE READING

Isaiah 43:1,10-11, 15; 44:6, 24.

v1 – But now saith <u>the LORD that created thee</u>, O Jacob, and <u>he that formed thee</u>, O Israel, Fear not: <u>for I have redeemed thee, I have called thee by thy name; thou art mine.</u>

....

v10 – Ye are <u>my </u>witnesses, saith <u>the LORD</u>, and <u>my</u> servant whom <u>I</u> have chosen: that ye may know and believe <u>me</u>, and understand that <u>I am he: before me there was no God formed, neither shall there be after me.</u>

v11 – <u>I, even I, and the LORD</u>; AND beside <u>me there is no savior.</u>

v15 – <u>I am the LORD, your Holy One, the creator of Israel, your King.</u>

....

Isaiah 44:6 – Thus saith the LORD the King of Israel, and his redeemer <u>the LORD of hosts; I am the first, and I am the last; and beside me there is no God.</u>

....

Isaiah 44:24 – Thus saith <u>the LORD</u>, thy <u>redeemer,</u> and <u>he </u>that formed thee from the womb, <u>I am the LORD</u> that maketh all things; that stretcheth forth the heavens <u>alone</u>; that spreadeth abroad the earth by <u>myself.</u>

....

NOTE: THE GOD WHO SPOKE TO PROPHET ISAIAH WAS <u>THE CREATOR</u> OF HEAVEAN AND EARTH. IN THE LATER CHAPTERS OF THIS BOOK, WE WILL FIND OUT THAT HE WAS <u>JESUS, THE ONLY GOD FROM ETERNITY</u>.

If you do not understand <u>the Scripture Reading</u> about the conversation between GOD and Prophet Isaiah, where GOD was telling the Prophet that <u>He alone created heaven and earth</u>, thus you will fail to understand the Contradiction by the New Testament authors like John and Paul.

Please read the SCRIPTURE READING carefully and prayerfully. Some may need to read it more than twice to grasp the truth before you go any further from here.

Failure to understand the Scripture Reading given above from the Book of Isaiah, will lead to your downfall of not understanding this GOD (ELOHIM) who created heaven and earth in six days and rested on the seventh day – (Genesis 1:1-31, 2:1-3).

INTRODUCTION

Imagine, you were standing in a <u>Book Store</u>, browsing at the <u>New Books</u> that were just being placed on the shelf. And suddenly, your eyes glaring at this Book.

While staring at <u>the Title</u> of this Book that says - "GOD DID NOT HAVE A BEGOTTEN SON," you got mixed feelings. Your mind hits the 10 miles per minute speed button. Question after question, bombarding your hard drive. What the heck? Who wrote that Hilarious, Contradicting, Satanic, Heretical Book?????????????????????????

Who would write such a Book? Did he *not* read John 3:16? What happened to the author's mind??????????????? Curiosity and unanswered questions stormed your mind.

Then, you paused and asked – Really? Did GOD give birth to a begotten Son called JESUS, in heaven? Or Did GOD create a begotten Son, in heaven?

Okay, whatever.???????

Is it possible that the Author is Correct??????????????????????? ....

Then, you paused, stopped looking at the Book; and now, picking up the Book, and started browsing the TABLE OF CONTENTS; and then quickly reading the INTRODUCTION and the CONCLUSION. Wow! That's me being mentioned by the author, you said to yourself.

Ten minutes later, you found yourself in the line toward the <u>Cashier</u>. You swiped your Credit Card and purchased the Book. You decided to go home and make time to read it. . . . Could the author be correct? If yes, then he has challenged the Scholars and Mainline Denominational Leaders to rethink and change their false teachings about JESUS. It's time to re-educate the Churches, Pastors, Bishops, Evangelists, Elders, and Professed Christians, on "HOW TO READ AND INTERPRET SCRIPTURE." Surely, The Theological Seminaries need a New Curriculum to teach Students and Pastors. It is going to be a New Reformation and Revival for the 21st Century. It is about JESUS, THE ONLY GOD IN HEAVEN. HE gave his own life. HE <u>did not</u> send a Son to die because <u>there was no Son of GOD in heaven</u>.

Books and Songs must be re-written to reflect the only one true GOD who gave his own life to die at Calvary.

....

Dear Reader, Thank you for your open mind in inquiring further. Believe me, your <u>curiosity</u> will be rewarded. Because you, like me, like to prove things. Many people don't inquire to learn something they did not know, thus their knowledge about GOD remain stagnant because their Denominations BRAINWASHED them.

KEEP THIS IN MIND. Truth is Progressive. Whether the people believe it or not, that does not stop you and me from probing deeper into the unsearched truths and new Revelations. Think of your own experience where you had believed in something as correct, but later learned that it was wrong, and had to abandon it. Have you had an experience like that? . . . I had. Many times. For example,

1. I used to believe that Sunday was the Sabbath. Later, I learned that Saturday was the Sabbath. Therefore, I had to abandon the Sunday Sabbath belief and became a Seventh-day Adventist member in 1972.

In 2021, I wrote a Book about the True Sabbath, which is Saturday, not Sunday.

2. I used to believe that we inherited Adam's sin. Later, I found out that sin is a choice, <u>not</u> by inheritance.

3. I used to believe that Babies Are Born Sinners. Later, I found out that Babies are <u>not</u> born sinners. Thus, I wrote the Book in 2011: 15 Reasons Babies Aren't Born Sinners.

Even though the Seventh-day Adventist Church still believes in "Babies Are Born Sinners", I chose <u>not</u> to compromise the truth.

Most mainline Denominations believe the False doctrine called – "Babies Are Born Sinners". And in 2021, I wrote another Book to counteract the False teaching.

4.   I used to believe in the <u>Trinity GOD theory</u>, but later discovered in my own study that JESUS was and is the only GOD, thus wrote three Books about JESUS.

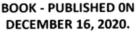

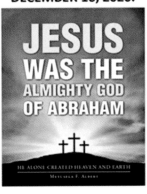
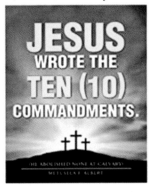
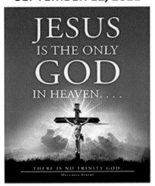

5.   I have many more to tell, but for now, let's concentrate on this Book – "GOD DID NOT HAVE A BEGOTTEN SON." This is going to be my 12TH BOOK.

6.   The Books can be ordered through – www.xlibris.com . . . www. amazon.com.

Dear Sir / Madam, . . . Please, stay tuned while you are reading this Book. GOD allowed you to find this Book which was designed for you and many others who are searching for the TRUTH about JESUS. Your faith will be rewarded with New Revelations that have <u>not</u> told to you yet. You don't need a Theological degree to understand it.

Please Check the "TABLE OF CONTENTS," and see if there is any Chapter in the Book where it speaks of something you did <u>not</u> know yet. Those Chapters were created to help prove the point of the TITLE of the Book.

I repeat again: The Truth will always be the Truth, whether the people believe it or not.

This Book you are holding in your hand was written to help believers in JESUS, worship Him, the One True GOD.

THERE WAS NO GOD BEFORE JESUS, AND NONE AFTER HIM. HE WAS, AND IS, THE ONLY GOD. THEREFORE, WE NEED TO STRONGLY CONDEMN THE TRINITY GOD THEORY WHICH PROMOTES AN IDOL GOD AGAINST JESUS CHRIST.

THE TRINITY GOD THEORY IS ANTI-CHRIST.

HOW?

The <u>Trinity</u> GOD theory promotes the idea that JESUS cannot be GOD by himself; for he must be <u>added to</u> <u>another Two Divine Beings</u>; <u>the Father and the Holy Spirit, to make one GOD.</u>

They call it – "THREE IN ONE."

1 + 1 + 1 = 1 GOD.

THE TRINITY GOD THEORY IS ANTI-CHRIST.

,,

....

LET'S READ - John 4:23-24.

JESUS said to the Samaritan woman,

v.23. But the hour cometh, and now is, when the <u>true worshipers</u> shall worship <u>the Father</u> in spirit and in truth: for <u>the Father</u> seeketh such to worship <u>him</u>.

v.24. God is a Spirit, and they that worship <u>him</u> must worship <u>him</u> <u>in spirit and in truth</u>."

NOTE: Worship the Father. . . Worship "<u>him</u>," not worship "them." There is no such thing called – TRINITY GOD OR TRIUNE GOD.

*** Check out the <u>singular male pronoun</u> used in John 4:23 & 24 – "him," NOT "them."

FIND OUT –

1.   WHO was <u>the Father</u>, in heaven?

....

2.   Was the Father, the GOD of Abraham, OR the Son of Abraham's GOD?

....

3.   Who was the GOD of Abraham?

....

4.   Was the GOD of Abraham, a Trinity GOD?

....

In John 4:25-26, JESUS gives us the answer to the above questions. We will hear it from the right person.

//////////////

LET'S READ - John 4:25-26.

v 25. The woman saith unto <u>him</u>, I know that Messias cometh, <u>which is called Christ</u>: when <u>he</u> is come, <u>he</u> will tell us all things.

v 26. Jesus saith unto her, <u>I that speak unto thee am he</u>.

NOTE: JESUS told the Samaritan woman at the well that He was the expected Messiah to come.

THE TRUTH IS: JESUS was the "ELOHIM" who created all things, and Adam and Eve in the Garden of Eden, who later came in human flesh to die at Calvary as our Savior.

JESUS was <u>NOT</u> the Son of GOD when He made heaven and earth because GOD had <u>no</u> begotten Son before He created the angels in heaven.

NOTE: The Son of God, and the Holy Spirit as a third person, <u>did not</u> exist in heaven.

THE BELIEF THAT SAYS, "GOD THE FATHER, GOD THE SON, AND GOD THE HOLY SPIRIT, ALL THREE EXISTED IN HEAVEN AS DISTINCT PERSONS" –

IS BALONEY AND SATANIC.

THE TRUTH WILL ALWAYS REMAIN THE TRUTH WHETHER THE PEOPLE BELIEVE IT OR NOT.

CHAPTER 1

THREE VIEWS ABOUT – THE FATHER, JESUS, AND THE HOLY SPIRIT.

- VIEW # 1. The GOD of Abraham was the only GOD, and JESUS was the Son of GOD. JESUS is the HOLY SPIRIT. The HOLY SPIRIT is <u>not</u> a third person. In this view, there are <u>TWO DISTINCT BEINGS, THE FATHER AND THE SON.</u>

....

- VIEW # 2. The FATHER, The SON, and The HOLY SPIRIT are <u>THREE DISTINCT Persons</u> that make <u>One GOD</u>. Expression is – "Three in One." . . . . 1 + 1 + 1 = 1 GOD.

- This is the teaching of the <u>TRINITY GOD</u> which is the <u>TRIUNE GOD</u> THEORY.

....

VIEW # 3. JESUS was, and is, the <u>only GOD</u>. HE was the FATHER who became the SON by the <u>INCARNATION</u> process through Mary at Bethlehem. The HOLY SPIRIT is the Spirit of JESUS, <u>not</u> a third person.

This View # 3 promotes only <u>ONE DIVINE BEING</u> that existed from eternity. HE was JESUS. It means, GOD did <u>not</u> have a Begotten Son, in heaven, before the angels were created.

- **This BOOK you are reading is focused on VIEW # 3.**

....

We, as followers of JESUS CHRIST, cannot afford to have all three views shared between different groups of believers without clarifying the correct View.

Most Christians believe in VIEW # 2. It is about the TRINITY GOD / TRIUNE GOD.

I understand that we are to respect the opinion of others; but I choose to respect GOD above all others. If others are teaching error, I choose to condemn their false doctrines. Condemning the false doctrines is <u>not</u> a disrespect to anyone. Allowing the false teachings to prevail, is a disrespect to JESUS, our only GOD who made us.

We have the truth written in <u>THE OLD TESTAMENT</u> about our <u>only GOD</u> (ELOHIM), who created heaven and earth, who delivered the children of Israel from slavery in Egypt, who wrote the Ten Commandments, who later came in human flesh by INCARNATION through Mary at Bethlehem and died at Calvary as our Savior, who is coming back again as the KING of all Kings.

We are to worship JESUS and give him the praise and glory due to him.

‹››

One of the three views mentioned above is correct, therefore, the other <u>two views</u> are wrong. We need to clarify the correct view and promote it aggressively to expose the errors. This Book is written for that purpose.

We as Christians must find out the correct view and <u>condemn the other two incorrect views</u> because having a false view about GOD is a mockery to Christianity. Did you realize that Commandment # 1 in the Ten

Commandments condemns the worship of false gods? And Commandment # 2 calls it - idol worship.

You already have your view, or perhaps you haven't, or maybe you are confused and don't know which is the correct view.

I urge you to stay tuned and keep reading till the end of the Book. You are going to learn the truth about the One <u>TRUE GOD in View # 3</u>.

....

This Book is written for the purpose to provoke our thoughts to analyze THE TRUTH about JESUS and establish it. Once THE TRUTH is established, the Error will be exposed.

THE TRUTH WILL CONDEMN THE FALSE TEACHING ABOUT - THE FATHER, THE SON, and THE HOLY SPIRIT, AS THREE DISTINCT PERSONS IN HEAVEN WHO MAKE UP ONE GOD.

"<u>THREE IN ONE</u>" IS THE <u>FAMOUS EXPRESSION</u> OF THE TRINITY GOD THEORY.

1 + 1 + 1 = 1 GOD.

THE FATHER + THE SON (JESUS) + THE HOLY SPIRIT = 1 TRINITY GOD.

NOTE: According to this theory, the <u>three persons</u> must combine to make <u>up one GOD</u>. Furthermore, JESUS cannot be GOD by himself simply because He has to be added to another TWO DIVINE BEINGS to make up one GOD. Therefore, JESUS could not be THE FIRST, AND THE LAST, neither THE ALPHA, AND OMEGA. . . .

THE TRINITY GOD CONCEPT CONTRADICTED WHAT GOD SAID ABOUT HIMSELF TO THE PROPHETS IN THE OLD TESTAMENT. . . .

(Please read the Scripture Reading - given in the beginning of the Book).

Re- read it and re-read it until you are clear that only <u>one GOD</u> created heaven and earth. Thus, NO TRINITY GOD created heaven and earth.

THREE DIFFERENT VIEWS ABOUT - GOD, JESUS, AND THE HOLY SPIRIT.

- #1. The God of Abraham was the only God, and JESUS was the begotten Son of God. Both existed from eternity. JESUS is the HOLY SPIRIT. Only TWO DISTINCT BEINGS.

- #2. The Father, The Son, The Holy Spirit, are <u>THREE DISTINCT PERSONS</u> that make one God. NOTE: The Expression is – "Three in One". . . . . .   1 + 1 + 1 = 1 God. . . . The Father sent his only begotten Son to die at Calvary as our Savior. And the Holy Spirit replaced JESUS on earth, after his ascension back to heaven. This is the teaching of the "TRINITY GOD" also called "TRIUNE GOD." Another expression is = God the Father + God the Son + God the Holy Spirit = 1 God.
- NOTE: Most Professed Christians and mainline Denominations believe in this Theory.

- #3. JESUS was, and is, the only God. He was the Father who became the Son by *incarnation* through Mary at Bethlehem. NOTE: The Holy Spirit is the Spirit of God which is the Spirit of JESUS. The Holy Spirit is <u>not</u> a third person. Only ONE DIVINE BEING in heaven from eternity. God did not have a begotten Son in heaven.
- * * * I used to believe in the Trinity, View #2. But no more. I now believe in view #3.

Compiled by: Metusela F. Albert. – Dated 08/17/2024.

....

Before you read CHAPTER 2 of this Book, make sure you read the Scripture Reading from the Book of Isaiah, as given above.

....

CHAPTER 2

JESUS WAS THE "ELOHIM" WHO CREATED HEAVEN AND EARTH.

Scripture Reading: Genesis 1:1. KJV

"In the beginning <u>GOD</u> (ELOHIM) created the heaven and the earth".

The <u>Hebrew word</u> used for the English word "<u>GOD</u>" in Genesis 1:1 is – "ELOHIM." It is in plural form.

....

WHO CREATED HEAVEN AND EARTH?

1. Was it "GOD", OR (2) "The Son of GOD", OR (3) The Father, The Son, and The Holy Spirit?

The correct answer is: # 1. "GOD" created heaven and earth.

NOTE: The Son of GOD did <u>not</u> create heaven and earth because there was <u>no Son of GOD</u> during the Creation time. GOD did <u>not</u> have a Son in heaven.

LET'S REPEAT AGAIN TO MAKE SURE THE READER GETS IT.

The Son of GOD did <u>not</u> create heaven and earth. Why? Because there was <u>no</u> person existed as - "Son of God," in heaven.

And the Holy Spirit was <u>not</u> a third person that existed in heaven. In heaven, there was only <u>one divine person called "GOD"</u>. HE was JESUS.

....

Let's read the <u>CONTEXT</u> in Genesis 1:27-31.

v.27. So <u>God</u> created man in <u>his</u> own image, in the image of <u>God</u> created <u>he</u> them.

v.28. And <u>God</u> blessed them, and <u>God</u> said unto them, Be fruitful and multiply, . . .

v.29. And <u>God</u> said, Behold, <u>I</u> have given you every herb bearing seed, which is upon the face of all the earth, and every tree in the which is fruit of a tree yielding seed; to you it shall be for meat.

v.30. And to every beast of the earth, and to every fowl of the air, and to everything that creepeth upon the earth, wherein there is life, <u>I</u> have given every green herb for meat: and it was so.

v.31. And <u>God</u> saw everything that <u>he had made</u>, and behold, it was very good. And the evening and the morning were the sixth day.

....

NOTE: DID YOU NOTICE <u>THE SINGULAR PRONOUNS</u> IN GENESIS 1:27-31?

....

LET'S FURTHER READ THE CONTEXT ABOUT "THE ELOHIM" WHO CREATED HEAVEN AND EARTH, IN GENESIS 2:1-3.

v.1. Thus the heavens and the earth were finished, and all the host of them,

v.2. And on the seventh day <u>God</u> ended <u>his</u> work which <u>he</u> hath made, and <u>he</u> rested on the seventh day from all <u>his</u> work which <u>he</u> had made.

v.3. And <u>God</u> blessed the seventh day and sanctified it: because that in it <u>he</u> had rested from all <u>his</u> work which <u>God</u> created and made.

....

CHECK OUT <u>THE SINGULAR PRONOUNS</u> USED IN GENESIS 2:1-3.

<u>The Pronoun</u> "His" = 3 Times, The Pronoun "He" = 4 Times. TOTAL 7.

POINT # 1 - THE GOD WHO RESTED ON THE SEVENTH DAY WAS *NOT* A TRINITY GOD.

POINT # 2 - JESUS WHO WAS THE LORD OF THE SABBATH DAY WAS *NOT* A TRINITY GOD.

....

After creating heaven and earth in six days, <u>GOD</u> rested on the seventh day. HE blessed the seventh day and hallowed it.

HE became "<u>the LORD</u>" of the Sabbath day. <u>HE was JESUS.</u>

....

BOTTOM LINE IS – JESUS WAS THE <u>"ELOHIM"</u> WHO CREATED HEAVEN AND EARTH IN SIX DAYS AND RESTED ON THE SABBATH.

THEREFORE, <u>JESUS WHO WAS</u> THE <u>"ELOHIM", THE FATHER OF THE CHILDREN OF ISRAEL,</u> DID <u>NOT</u> HAVE A SON CALLED JESUS, IN HEAVEN NEITHER IN THE OLD TESTAMENT ERA.

CHAPTER 3

HOW TO UNDERSTAND GENESIS 1:26.

....

SCRIPTURE: Genesis 1:26 –

[26] And God said, "Let <u>Us</u> make man in <u>Our</u> image, after <u>Our</u> likeness; and let them have dominion over the fish of the sea, and over the fowl of the air, and over the cattle, and over all the earth and over every creeping thing that creepeth upon the earth."

....

NOTE: Genesis 1:26 is the *first text* that is being <u>misinterpreted</u> by most Professed Christians and Mainline Denominations (Churches), to justify the <u>Trinity GOD</u> theory.

This is the first verse that deceived so many millions to believe in a Trinity GOD theory because they failed to understand *the Context* in Genesis 1:27-31 and Genesis 2:1-3.

Okay, let's try and understand Genesis 1:26 to counteract the misinterpretation error made by those who believe the TRINITY doctrine.

Let's ask a few questions to bring out the meaning stated in Genesis 1:26.

Question # 1. Who was GOD <u>speaking to</u> when GOD said, "Let <u>us</u> make man in <u>our</u> image after <u>our</u> likeness . . . ?"

ANSWER # 1: Possibly, GOD was talking to the angel called – "GABRIEL" - (Luke 1:19). He was the angel that spoke to Zacharias, the father of John the Baptist. The same angel spoke to Mary and informed her that she was conceived by the power of the Holy Spirit – (Luke 1:26). Even though she never had sex with a man, yet she was pregnant. That is the INCARNATION by the power of GOD. . . .

Angel GABRIEL also told Mary, the name of the child to be born – "JESUS".

....

....

Question # 2: What was the IMAGE of GOD? . . . "SINLESSNESS." GOD IS SINLESS. The angels were created by God as <u>Sinless Beings</u>, in heaven.

1.   Unless we know <u>WHO, GOD was speaking to</u>, we will <u>not</u> understand Genesis 1:26.

2.   What is GOD'S Image? . . . SINLESSNESS.

3.   <u>GOD IS SINLESS</u>, and the angels in heaven were created SINLESS after GOD'S image.

4.   <u>Thus,</u> Adam and Eve were to be created SINLESS, after GOD'S Image.

5.   REMEMBER, whosoever GOD was talking to in Genesis 1:26, had GOD'S image which is <u>SINLESSNESS</u>.

6.   In Genesis 1:26, GOD was going to create Adam and Eve in <u>His own Image</u>.

7.   In Genesis 1:27, GOD created Adam and Eve in <u>His Image</u>, which is <u>SINLESSNESS</u>.

8. After creating Adam and Eve on <u>the sixth day</u>, GOD rested on <u>the seventh day</u> – Genesis 2:1-3. Take note of <u>the Singular Pronouns</u> used – "His" and "He."

9. GOD alone created Adam and Eve, and everything. (Genesis 1:27-31).

10. None of the unfallen angels created Adam and Eve.

11. The unfallen angel Gabriel did NOT create Adam and Eve.

12. <u>There was no such thing as the Father, the Son, and the Holy Spirit, co-created heaven and earth.</u>

13. And there was <u>no</u> such thing as the Father and the Son, co-created heaven and earth because GOD did NOT have a Begotten Son in heaven before the angels existed.

<hr>

THE "ELOHIM" OF THE SABBATH DAY WAS <u>NOT</u> A TRINITY GOD. (Read the "Singular Pronouns").

- Genesis 2:1-3 (King James Version).
- 1. Thus the heavens and the earth were finished, and all the host of them.
- 2 And on the seventh day God ended <u>His</u> work which <u>He</u> had made; and <u>He</u> rested on the seventh day from all <u>His</u> work which <u>He</u> had made.
- 3 And <u>God</u> blessed the seventh day and sanctified it, because in it <u>He</u> had rested from all <u>His</u> work which <u>God</u> created and made.

Compiled by: Metusela F. Albert

<hr>

Most people and Churches failed to read the context of Genesis 1:26 in Genesis Chapter 1:1-25, and Genesis 1:27-31, and Genesis 2:1-3.

That is why they continued to believe in a FALSE TRINITY GOD theory.

They missed understanding the SINGULAR PRONOUNS used.

....

CHAPTER 4

JESUS WAS THE GOD OF NOAH AND HIS FAMILY.

....

SCRIPTURE – Genesis 6:1-22.

¹And it came to pass, when men began to multiply on the face of the earth and daughters were born unto them,

² that the sons of God saw the daughters of men, that they were fair; and they took for themselves wives of all whom they chose.

³ And <u>the Lord said</u>, "<u>My</u> Spirit shall not always strive with man, for he also is flesh; <u>yet his days shall be a hundred and twenty years</u>."

⁴ There were giants on the earth in those days; and also after that, when the sons of <u>God</u> came in unto the daughters of men and they bore children to them, the same became mighty men who were of old, men of renown.

⁵ And <u>God</u> saw that the wickedness of man was great in the earth, and that every imagining of the thoughts of his heart was only evil continually.

⁶ And <u>the Lord</u> repented that <u>He</u> had made man on the earth, and it grieved <u>Him</u> in <u>His</u> heart.

⁷ And <u>the Lord</u> said, "<u>I</u> will destroy man whom <u>I</u> have created from the face

of the earth, both man and beast, and the creeping thing and the fowls of the air, <u>for I repent that I have made them</u>."

8 But Noah found grace in the eyes of <u>the Lord</u>.

9 These are the generations of Noah. Noah was a just man and perfect in his generations, and Noah walked with <u>God.</u>

10 And Noah begot three sons: Shem, Ham, and Japheth.

11 The earth also was corrupt before <u>God</u>, and the earth was filled with violence.

12 And <u>God</u> looked upon the earth, and behold, it was corrupt; for all flesh had corrupted his way upon the earth.

13 And <u>God</u> said unto Noah, "The end of all flesh has come before <u>Me</u>, for the earth is filled with violence through them; and behold, <u>I</u> will destroy them with the earth.

14 Make thee an ark of gopherwood; rooms shalt thou make in the ark, and shalt cover it within and without with pitch.

15 And this is the fashion which thou shalt make it of: the length of the ark shall be three hundred cubits, the breadth of it fifty cubits, and the height of it thirty cubits.

16 A window shalt thou make for the ark, and to a cubit shalt thou finish it above; and the door of the ark shalt thou set in the side thereof; with lower, second, and third stories shalt thou make it.

17 And behold, I, even I, do bring a flood of waters upon the earth to destroy all flesh wherein is the breath of life from under heaven; and every thing that is on the earth shall die.

18 But with thee will <u>I</u> establish <u>My</u> covenant; and thou shalt come into the ark, thou and thy sons, and thy wife and thy sons' wives with thee.

¹⁹ And of every living thing of all flesh, two of every sort shalt thou bring into the ark to keep them alive with thee; they shall be male and female.

²⁰ Of fowls after their kind, and of cattle after their kind, of every creeping thing of the earth after his kind, two of every sort shall come unto thee to keep them alive.

²¹ And take thou unto thee of all food that is eaten, and thou shalt gather it to thee; and it shall be food for thee and for them."

²² Thus did Noah; according to all that <u>God</u> commanded him, <u>so did he.</u>

....

THERE ARE 22 verses in Genesis Chapter 6 about GOD'S CONVERSATION WITH NOAH; FOR HIM TO BUILD AN ARK IN PREPARATION FOR THE FLOOD.

PLEASE TAKE TIME TO READ THIS CHAPTER, AND MARK "<u>THE SINGULAR PRONOUNS USED FOR THE WORD - GOD.</u>"

....

JESUS WHO WAS THE GOD WHO CREATED HEAVEN AND EARTH, <u>SPOKE TO NOAH</u> TO BUILD AN ARK BEFORE THE FLOOD.

DID YOU NOTICE IT?

THE GOD OF NOAH WAS <u>NOT</u> A TRINITY GOD.

....

THE GOD OF NOAH WAS <u>NOT</u> A TRINITY GOD. HE WAS JESUS, THE ELOHIM, WHO CREATED HEAVEN AND EARTH IN SIX DAYS.

- Genesis 6:5-7 (King James Version).

- [5] And <u>God</u> saw that the wickedness of man was great in the earth, and that every imagining of the thoughts of his heart was only evil continually.

- [6] And <u>the Lord</u> repented that <u>He</u> had made man on the earth, and it grieved <u>Him</u> in <u>His</u> heart.

- [7] And <u>the Lord</u> said, "<u>I</u> will destroy man whom <u>I</u> have created from the face of the earth, both man and beast, and the creeping thing and the fowls of the air, for <u>I</u> repent that <u>I</u> have made them."

- ....

- NOTE: PLEASE READ THE SINGULAR PRONOUNS USED IN THE THREE VERSES SHOWN ABOVE. THAT WAS <u>NOT</u> A TRINITY GOD.

Compiled by: Metusela F. Albert.

CHAPTER 5

JESUS WAS THE "GOD" OF ABRAHAM.

SCRIPTURE Reading: Genesis 12:1-4.

v1. Now <u>the LORD</u> hath said unto Abram, Get thee out of thy country, and from thy kindred, and from thy father's house, unto a land that <u>I</u> will shew thee:

v2. <u>And I</u> will make of thee a great nation, <u>and I</u> will bless thee, and make thy name great, and thou shalt be a blessing:

v3. <u>And I</u> will bless them that bless thee and curse him that curseth thee: and in thee shall all families of the earth be blessed.

v4. So, Abram <u>departed</u>, as <u>the LORD</u> had spoken to him: and Lot went with him: and Abram was <u>seventy and five years old</u> when he <u>departed</u> out of Haran.

....

THE GOD OF ABRAHAM WAS NOT A TRINITY GOD. (Read the Singular Pronouns).

- **Scripture Reading: Genesis 12:1-4.**
- v1. Now <u>the LORD</u> hath said unto Abram, Get thee out of thy country, and from thy kindred, and from thy father's house, unto a land that <u>I</u> will shew thee:
- v2. And <u>I</u> will make of thee a great nation, and <u>I</u> will bless thee, and make thy name great, and thou shalt be a blessing:
- v3. And <u>I</u> will bless them that bless thee and curse him that curseth thee: and in thee shall all families of the earth be blessed.

  v4. So Abram <u>departed</u>, as <u>the LORD</u> had spoken to him: and Lot went with him: and Abram was <u>seventy and five years old</u> when he <u>departed</u> out of Haran.

NOTE: THE PRONOUN "I" WAS MENTIONED 4 TIMES.

Compiled by: Metusela F. Albert.

....

The first three verses of Genesis Chapter 12 used the <u>Singular Pronoun –</u> <u>"I" four times</u> to refer to GOD who spoke to Abraham.

Therefore, the GOD of Abraham was <u>not</u> a TRINITY GOD.

FURTHER EVIDENCE / PROOF.

In the New Testament, JESUS said:

John 5:39 – "<u>Search the Scriptures</u>; for in them ye think ye have eternal life: and <u>they are they which testify of me</u>."

....

John 5:46 – "For had ye believed Moses, ye would have believed <u>me</u>: for <u>he</u> <u>wrote of me</u>."

....

Moses wrote 5 Books: Genesis, Exodus, Leviticus, Numbers, Deuteronomy in the Hebrew language.

....

NOTE: THE JEWS CLAIMED TO BELIEVE IN MOSES AND THE GOD OF ABRAHAM. BUT THEY FAILED TO UNDERSTAND THAT JESUS WHO CAME IN HUMAN FLESH WAS THE GOD OF ABRAHAM THAT MOSES WROTE IN <u>THE FIRST FIVE BOOKS OF THE HEBREEW BIBLE, THE TORAH.</u>

LET'S READ: John 8:56-58 – AND LOOK AT ANOTHER EVIDENCE / PROOF.

v.56 – Your father Abraham rejoiced to see my day: and he saw it, and was glad.

v57 – Then said the Jews unto him, Thou art not yet fifty years old, and hast seen Abraham?

v.58 – Jesus said unto them, "Verily, verily, I say unto you, <u>Before Abraham was, I am.</u>"

....

NOTE: JESUS told the unbelieving Jews that HE existed before their father Abraham. Unfortunately, they failed to understand his intended meaning in verse 58.

- JESUS was trying to make them understand that HE was <u>the GOD</u> of Abraham whom Moses wrote in the <u>PENTATEUCH</u> – Genesis, Exodus, Leviticus, Numbers, Deuteronomy.

- Sadly, they killed him through the Romans and fulfilled the Prophecy written in Isaiah 53:1-10. His own Jewish people rejected and killed him.

//

. . . .

DON'T MISS THE POINT OF THIS BOOK.

Since JESUS was the GOD of Abraham, hence, HE was <u>not</u> the Son of Abraham's GOD.

That is the reason "GOD did <u>*not*</u> have a Begotten Son called JESUS, in heaven."

Furthermore: And the Holy Spirit was <u>not</u> a person nor a third person in heaven.

CHAPTER 6

JESUS WAS THE "JEHOVAH" OF MOSES AND THE ISRAELITES.

SCRIPTURE Reading: Exodus 3:13-15; 6:1-3, 7.

v13. – And Moses said unto <u>God</u>, Behold, when I come unto the children of Israel, and shall say unto them, The <u>God</u> of your fathers hath sent me unto you; and they shall say to me, What is his name? What shall I say unto them?

v14. And <u>God</u> said unto Moses, <u>I AM THAT I AM</u>: and he said, Thus shalt thou say unto the children of Israel, <u>I AM</u> hath sent me unto you.

V15. And <u>God</u> said moreover unto Moses, Thus shalt thou say unto the children of Israel, <u>The LORD God</u> of your fathers, <u>the God of Abraham</u>, <u>the God of Isaac</u>, and <u>the God of Jacob</u>, hath sent me unto you: <u>this is my name forever</u>, and this is my memorial for all generations.

....

Exodus 6:1-3, 7. THE NAME <u>JEHOVAH</u>.

v1. Then <u>the LORD said</u> unto Moses, Now shalt thou see what <u>I</u> will do to Pharoah: for with a strong hand shall he let them go, and with a strong hand shall he drive them out of his land.

v2. And <u>God</u> spake unto Moses, and said unto him, <u>I am the LORD</u>.

v3. And I appeared unto Abraham, unto Isaac, and unto Jacob, by the name of God Almighty, but by my name JEHOVAH was I not known to them.

v7. And I will take you to me for a people, and I will be to you a God: and ye shall know that I am the LORD your God, which bringeth you out from under the burdens of the Egyptians.

………………………………………………………………………………

DID YOU NOTICE THE SINGULAR PRONOUNS USED IN THE ABOVE SCRIPTURE?

THAT GOD WHO SPOKE TO MOSES WAS NOT A TRINITY GOD.

NOTE: LISTED BELOW ARE SOME OF THE VARIOUS NAMES OR TITLES, HOW GOD WAS ADDRESSED IN THE OLD TESTAMENT.

GOD = I AM THAT I AM = I AM = The LORD Almighty = JEHOVAH = The GOD of Abraham = The GOD of Isaac = The GOD of Jacob = The GOD of the children of Israel = The Creator = The Redeemer = The Savior = The Holy ONE = The KING of Israel = The Most HIGH, The Angel of the LORD, ETC.

………………………………………………………………………………

JESUS WAS THE "I AM THAT I AM" THAT SPOKE TO MOSES AT THE BURNING BUSH – (Exodus 3:13-14).

Read John 5:39, 46.

Read John 8:56-58.

JESUS WAS ALSO CALLED – "THE LORD GOD ALMIGHTY", and "JEHOVAH".

Since JESUS was the "JEHOVAH" of Moses and the children of Israel,

therefore, it is proven that "JEHOVAH" did <u>not</u> have a Son called JESUS, in heaven, before the angels were created.

NOTE: Most Professed Christians and Mega Denominations still have not understood what you just read above. Because they haven't understood it, that is why they still believe in a Trinity God theory with three persons existing in heaven. They believed in John's Duality God in John 1:1. They had to believe in the <u>Duality God</u> theory, first, in order to proceed to the Trinity God theory in 1 John 5:7.

Of course, most Professed Christians and mainline Denominations (Churches) had no idea of the Contradictions by John and Paul in their beliefs about (1) THE FATHER, (2) JESUS, AND (3) THE HOLY SPIRIT.

Please stay tuned and keep reading to the end of the Book.

....

CHAPTER 7

JESUS WAS THE "I AM" WHO WROTE THE TEN COMMANDMENTS.

SCRIPTURE Reading: Exodus 3:13-14,

v13. And Moses said unto God, Behold, when I come unto the children of Israel, and shall say unto them, The God of your fathers hath sent me unto you; and they shall say to me, what is his name? What shall I say unto them?

v14. And God said unto Moses, <u>I AM THAT I AM</u>: and he said, Thus shalt thou say unto the children of Israel, <u>I AM</u> hath sent me unto you.

SCRIPTURE: Exodus 20:1-3.

v1. And <u>God</u> spake all these words, saying,

v2. <u>I am the LORD thy God</u>, which have brought the out of the land of Egypt, out of the house of bondage.

v3. Thou shalt have no other gods before me.

....

John 5:39.

Jesus said, "Search ye the Scriptures; for in them ye think ye have eternal life, but they are they which testify of <u>me</u>."

John 5:46.

Jesus said, "For had ye believed Moses, ye would have believed <u>me:</u> for <u>Moses wrote of me.</u>"

John 5:47 – But if ye believe not his writings, how shall ye believe <u>my</u> words?

SCRIPTURE: John 8:56-58.

Jesus said,

v 56. Your father Abraham rejoiced to see <u>my</u> day: and he saw it and was glad.

v 57. Then said the Jews unto him, Thou art <u>not yet fifty years old</u>, and <u>hast thou seen Abraham?</u>

v 58. <u>Jesus said unto them, Verily, verily, I say unto you, Before Abraham was I am.</u>

....

LET'S READ REVELATION 21:6-7, TO UNDERSTAND THAT THIS GOD WHO SPOKE TO JOHN ON THE ISLAND OF PATMOS WAS THE SAME GOD WHO SPOKE TO MOSES AND THE PROPHETS IN THE OLD TESTAMENT.

SCRIPTURE: REVELATION 21:6-7.

v 6. – And <u>he</u> said unto me(John), It is done. <u>I am Alpha and Omega, the beginning and the end.</u> <u>I</u> will give unto him that is athirst of the fountain of the water of life freely.

v 7. – He that overcometh shall inherit all things; and <u>I</u> will be his God, and he shall be my Son.

....

THE GOD CALLED – "I AM THAT I AM, AND ALPHA AND OMEGA", WAS JESUS WHO CAME IN HUMAN FLESH THROUGH MARY AND DIED AT CALVARY, TO SAVE MANKIND FROM SIN.

JESUS, WAS AND IS, THE ONLY GOD IN HEAVEN. HE WAS THE GOD OF ABRAHAM, ISAAC, AND JACOB.

HE DID <u>NOT</u> HAVE A SON IN HEAVEN CALLED JESUS.

CHAPTER 8

JESUS WAS THE "ELOHIM" OF PROPHET ISAIAH.

SCRIPTURE: Reading: Isaiah 43:10-11, 15; 44:6, 24; 49:16.

Isaiah 43:3, 10-11, 15

v.3. For <u>I am the LORD thy God</u>, <u>the Holy One of Israel, thy Savior:</u> . . .

v.10. Ye are <u>my</u> witnesses, <u>saith the LORD</u>, and <u>my</u> servant whom <u>I</u> have chosen: that ye may know and believe <u>me</u>, and understand that <u>I am he:</u> before <u>me</u> <u>there was no God formed</u>, <u>neither shall there be after me.</u>

<u>v.11. I, even I, am the LORD; and beside me there is no saviour.</u>

v.15. <u>I am the LORD, your Holy One, the creator of Israel, your King.</u>

READ - Isaiah 44:6, 8, 24.

v6. Thus saith <u>the LORD</u> the King of Israel, and <u>his redeemer the LORD of hosts; I am the first, and I am the last; and beside me there is no God.</u>

v8. . . . Is there a God beside me? Yea, <u>there is no God: I know not any.</u>

v.24.Thus saith <u>the LORD</u>, thy redeemer, and <u>he that formed thee</u> from the womb, <u>I am the LORD</u> that <u>maketh all things;</u> that <u>stretcheth forth the heavens</u> <u>alone;</u> that spreadeth abroad the earth <u>by myself.</u>

Isaiah 49:16 – Behold, <u>I have graven thee upon the palms of my hands</u>; thy walls are continually before <u>me.</u>

....

Isaiah 9:6.

For unto us a child is born, unto us a son is given: and the government shall be upon his shoulder: and <u>his name shall be called</u> <u>Wonderful, Counsellor, The mighty God, The everlasting Father, the Prince of Peace.</u>

Isaiah 7:14. Therefore, the Lord himself shall give you a sign; Behold, <u>a virgin</u> shall conceive, and bear a son, and shall call his name <u>Immanuel</u>.

....

Matthew 1:20-23 – IMMANUEL means GOD WITH US.

v.20. But while he thought on these things, behold, <u>the angel of the Lord appeared unto him in a dream</u> saying, Joseph, thou son of David, fear not to take unto thee Mary thy wife: for that which is conceived in her is of the Holy Ghost.

v.21. And she shall bring forth a son, and thou shalt call his name <u>JESUS</u>: for he shall save his people <u>from</u> their sins.

v.22. Now all this was done, that it might be fulfilled which was spoken of the Lord by the prophet, saying,

<u>v.23. Behold, a virgin shall be with child, and shall bring forth a son, and they shall call his name Emmanuel, which being interpreted is, God with us.</u>

NOTE: GOD JEHOVAH TOOK HUMAN FLESH AND WAS CALLED JESUS. HE WAS THE EMMANUEL PROPHESIED IN THE BOOK OF ISAIAH, GOD WITH US. . . YEA, JESUS WAS THE JEHOVAH OF MOSES WHO BECAME HUMAN THROUGH MARY AT BETHLEHM.

DID YOU NOTICE THAT THE GOD OF PROPHET ISAIAH WAS THE SAME GOD WHO CREATED HEAVEN AND EARTH? HE WAS "ELOHIM" IN GENESIS 1:1.

HE WAS THE "I AM THAT I AM", THE "JEHOVAH" WHO SPOKE TO MOSES AT THE BURNING BUSH. HE WAS THE GOD WHO DELIVERED THE CHILDREN OF ISRAEL FROM SLAVERY IN EGYPT. HE WROTE THE TEN COMMANDMENTS ON TWO TABLETS OF STONE AT MOUNT SINAI AND GAVE THROUGH MOSES FOR ALL MANKIND. HE WAS JESUS.

THERE IS ONLY <u>ONE GOD</u>, HE ALONE CREATED HEAVEN AND EARTH.

READ THE BOOK OF ISAIAH WELL AND LISTEN CAREFULLY TO <u>THE SINGULAR PRONOUNS</u> USED.

THE SCRIPTURES IN ISAIAH ARE LISTED ABOVE FOR YOUR UNDERSTANDING.

....

THE TRUTH versus THE ERROR.

THE TRUTH

- JESUS was the <u>Only GOD</u> from eternity. HE did not have a begotten Son.
- HE was the FATHER who became the Son by the Incarnation process through Mary at Bethlehem. <u>One Being</u>.
- The Holy Spirit is the Spirit of JESUS. . . The Holy Spirit is <u>not</u> a third person.

THE ERROR

- The Father, the Son, and the Holy Spirit, are <u>three distinct persons</u> that make up One GOD.
- 1 + 1 + 1 = 1 GOD.
- This is the Trinity GOD theory called Triune GOD.

Compiled by: Metusela F. Albert

According to the TRINITY GOD THEORY, JESUS who was ALPHA AND OMEGA, cannot be a self-existent GOD since He must be ADDED (COMBINED) <u>with TWO Divine Beings</u> called - the FATHER AND THE SON, to make up <u>One GOD</u>.

By now, you as a believer in JESUS CHRIST should have seen the SATANIC doctrine of the TRINITY GOD THEORY which degrades JESUS, a self-existed GOD, to a creature with a beginning in heaven; a begotten of the Father.

Sir / Madam, I adjure you by GOD'S grace, don't believe again in the lies of your Church, if your Church is teaching the TRINITY GOD theory which is the TRIUNE GOD theory.

Be a mature Christian that eats hard food, not drinking milk from a bottle. Show some maturity in your reasoning and thinking. Give GOD the glory.

Stay tuned and continue reading.

....

CHAPTER 9

JESUS WAS THE FIRST AND THE LAST, THE ALPHA AND OMEGA.

....

JESUS WAS "THE LORD GOD" OF KING DAVID AND KING SOLOMON.

SCRIPTURE Reading: Psalm 100:3 –

Know ye that <u>the LORD he is God</u>: <u>it is he that hath made us</u>, and not we ourselves; we are <u>his</u> people, and the sheep of his pasture.

NOTE: The GOD of King David was <u>the CREATOR of heaven and earth</u>. HE was the "ELOHIM" who made heaven and earth. HE was JESUS.

....

Proverbs 3:1 – <u>God</u> said Soloman, <u>My</u> son, forget <u>not my law</u>; but let thine heart keep <u>my</u> commandments."

NOTE: The JEHOVAH who wrote the Ten Commandments spoke to King Solomon and reminded him not to forget his commandments. The law of God is to be kept in his heart.

....

King Solomon wrote in Ecclesiastes 12:1.

"REMEMBER now <u>thy Creator</u> in the days of thy youth while the evil days come not, nor the years draw nigh, when thou shalt say, I have no pleasure in them."

....

NOTE: The GOD of King Solomon was the <u>ELOHIM</u> who created heaven and earth in six days and rested on the seventh day. HE WAS JESUS.

JESUS WAS <u>NOT</u> A TRINITY GOD. HE DID <u>NOT</u> HAVE "A SON CALLED JESUS", IN HEAVEN.

The GOD of King David was "<u>THE CREATOR</u>." HE was the "<u>ELOHIM</u>" who created heaven and earth. HE was JESUS.

In Psalms 23:1-3, David acknowledged "<u>the LORD</u>" as his Sheperd.

In John 10, JESUS said, "I am the good Shepherd." Yeah, JESUS was the good Shepherd, the LORD, of King David.

King Solomon, the son of King David, also trusted in the "CREATOR" of heaven and earth.

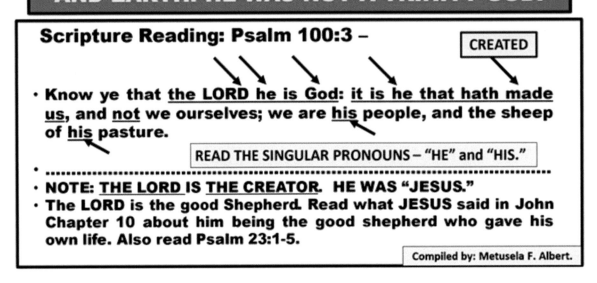

JESUS WAS THE FIRST AND THE LAST, THE ALPHA AND OMEGA.

SCRIPTURE Reading - Rev. 1:8; 4:8-11; 21:6-7.

CHAPTER 10

"ELOHIM" TOOK HUMAN FLESH AND DIED AT CALVARY. JOHN 14:6-9.

Genesis 1:1 – In the beginning God created the heaven and the earth.

....

In the Hebrew language, the word "Elohim" is used for the word "God" in Genesis 1:1. Elohim is in plural form.

<u>No English translation</u> says, In the beginning Gods created the heaven and the earth.

No Jewish person says, <u>the Gods</u> of Abraham, Isaac, and Jacob.

READ THE CONTEXT OF ELOHIM IN GENESIS 1:1-31.

The Pronoun Context tells of God, "he" in Genesis 1:5, 10, 16.

When you read the God of Noah in Genesis Chapter 6, he was <u>not</u> "<u>Gods</u>".

Likewise, when you read the God of Abraham in Genesis 12:1-3, he was <u>not</u> "<u>Gods</u>".

THE POINT IS: THERE WAS NOT SUCH THING A TRINITY GOD CREATED HEAVEN AND EARTH.

FURTHERMORE, JESUS WAS <u>NOT</u> A TRINITY GOD. HE WAS THE

ELOHIM **WHO CREATED HEAVEN AND EARTH IN SIX DAYS AND RESTED ON THE SEVENTH DAY.**

JESUS WAS ALSO CALLED - I AM THAT I AM, JEHOVAH, THE KING OF ALL KINGS, THE REDEEMER, THE SAVIOR, THE FIRST AND THE LAST, ALPHA AND OMEGA, ETC.

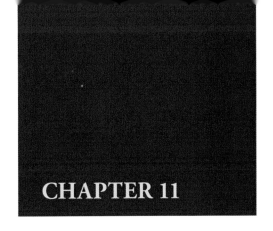

CHAPTER 11

THE TWO NATURES OF "ELOHIM" (JESUS) WHILE IN HUMAN FLESH.

When "ELOHIM," who created heaven and earth in six days condescended and took up human flesh through Mary at Bethlehem to die at Calvary as our Sin Offering to save mankind, he did _not_ cease from being GOD.

GOD is eternal and will always remain as GOD.

....

If there was a time that GOD was _not_ GOD, then GOD _cannot_ be GOD. That is why when GOD took human flesh, he was still GOD.

JESUS _veiled his divinity_ while in human flesh. No one with a mortal body with a sinful nature can see GOD'S divine glory and remain alive. JESUS did not cease to be GOD while he was in human flesh for thirty-three and a half years on earth. JESUS appeared in human flesh through the INCARNATION in Mary at Bethlehem, yet he was still GOD. HE veiled his Divine glory during his human presence on earth. His miracles proved his divinity but the Jews failed to recognize it.

Do You still remember? When GOD spoke to Moses at the burning bush, GOD did _not_ appear to him in His divine glory, as GOD. HE appeared <u>as a burning bush</u>, and GOD's voice was heard by Moses in his own language (the Hebrew language).

Remember? Moses wrote the first five books of the Old Testament in the Hebrew language.

ANOTHER EXAMPLE:

When GOD appeared to Abraham in the Plains of Mamre, while on his way with two angels to Sodom and Gomorrah, He appeared <u>as a man</u>. Abraham recognized them as three men. Then Abraham and his wife prepared a meal for them to eat. A calf was killed. Bread, Butter, and Milk were part of the meal. It was not a vegetarian nor a vegan meal.

GOD, as a man, <u>ate with Abraham</u>. Read the story in Genesis 18:1-8.

GOD cannot appear to Abraham and Sarah in his divine glory. Why? Because Abraham and Sarah would die if they saw His divine glory.

....

The subject about the "<u>TWO NATURES of JESUS</u>" is so vital for our understanding to understand that "GOD did <u>not</u> send a begotten Son from heaven to die at Calvary."

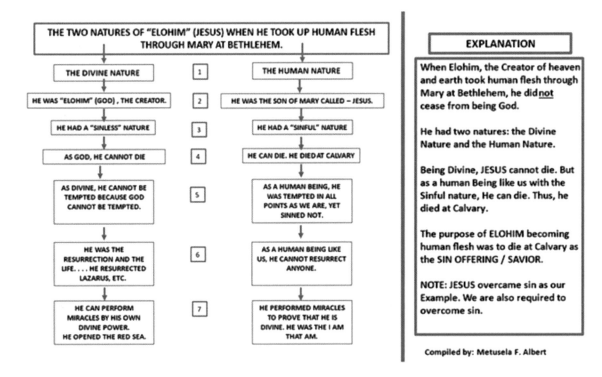

The Power Point slide diagram above explains the "TWO NATURES" of JESUS in a way that may help the reader to understand the subject much easier. I hope that helps your understanding.

CHAPTER 12

JOHN CONTRADICTED WHAT GOD SAID IN THE OLD TESTAMENT.

JOHN 1:1 <u>CONTRADICTED</u> WHAT GOD SAID IN THE OLD TESTAMENT.

2 JOHN 1:3, 9.

Scripture Reading – John 3:16-18, 35-36.

JESUS, in is his conversation with Mr. Nicodemus, said,

v.16. "For God so loved the world, that he gave his <u>only begotten Son</u>, that whosoever believeth in <u>him</u> should not perish, but have everlasting life." (KJV)

v.17. For <u>God</u> sent not <u>his Son</u> into the world to condemn the world; but that the world through <u>him</u> might be saved.

v.18. He that <u>believeth on him</u> is <u>not</u> condemned; but he that <u>believeth not</u> is condemned already, because he hath <u>not believed</u> in the name of the <u>only begotten Son of God.</u>

v.35. The <u>Father loveth the Son</u>, and hath given all things into <u>his</u> hand.

v.36. <u>He that believeth on the Son</u> hath everlasting life: and <u>he that believeth not the Son</u> shall not see life; but the wrath of God abideth on him.

....

According to JESUS who spoke the words recorded in John 3:16, he said -

1. God had a Son in heaven.

2. God sent the Son to earth.

3. The name of the Son was JESUS.

4. God the Father remained in heaven.

5. God the Father and the Son were <u>TWO DISTINCT (Separate)</u> Divine Beings.

6. They are <u>*not*</u> one Being.

7. He or she that believeth <u>not in</u> <u>the Son of God</u> called JESUS, has no everlasting life.

....

John 3:16 is the most memorized Scripture amongst Professed Christians in any generation. This is the *key text* that builds the foundation of God's unconditional love to save mankind.

This text advocates that God and his Son existed from eternity, before the angels existed.

According to John 3:16, God the Father and his begotten Son were <u>Two Distinct Divine Beings from eternity. Two? Yeah! That's what JESUS said.</u>

Well, let's read what John wrote in John 1:1-3 about God the Father and his Son.

John, wrote John 1:1. It says, "In the beginning was the Word, and the Word was <u>with</u> God, and the Word was God."

....

TWO DISTINCT GODS ADVOCATED BY JOHN.

God the Father + God the Son = 2 Gods. NOT 1 God.

The DUALITY God theory started by JESUS who spoke the words in John 3:16.

Perhaps, you did not realize it till this time, and that is okay because we learn things as we grow.

THINK AGAIN.

According to John, GOD the Father and GOD the Son, both existed from the beginning, and both were "TWO DISTINCT GODS."

The disciple John advocated the DUALITY GOD Theory in John 1:1.

John also advocated that GOD the Son created all things. Nothing that was created, was created without him. John 1:1-3.

When John talks about the CREATOR, he refers to JESUS, the Son of GOD. He was GOD the Son.

It shows that the disciple John at the time of writing, he did not know that JESUS who came in human flesh was the "ELOHIM" mentioned in Genesis 1:1 who created heaven and earth. Apparently, JESUS was *not* the Son of GOD at the time he created heaven and earth.

....

According to John 3:16, it was GOD the Father who sent his only begotten Son to die at Calvary, as the Sin Bearer / Savior.

According to John 3:16, GOD the Father remained in heaven, but GOD the Son came to earth as a human being like us, to die at Calvary as our Savior.

....

NOTE: According to John 1:1 and John 3:16, GOD the Father and GOD the Son were <u>TWO DISTINCT GODS</u> that existed in heaven from eternity before the angels existed. This Contradicted Isaiah 43:10-11.

///

JOHN 3:16 <u>CONTRADICTED</u> WHAT GOD SAID IN THE OLD TESTAMENT.

CHAPTER 13 -

PAUL CONTRADICTED THE OLD TESTAMENT.

CHAPTER 14 –

PETER CONTRADICTED WHAT GOD SAID IN THE OLD TESTAMENT. 1 PETER 1:3.

CHAPTER 15.

WHO WAS THE HOLY SPIRIT? NO THIRD PERSON IN HEAVEN.

CHAPTER 16 -

ELOHIM (YAHWEH / JEHOVAH) HAD NO BEGOTTEN SON, IN HEAVEN.

CHAPTER 17 -

CLARIFY MATTHEW 3:16-17 AND MATTHEW 28:19-20.

CHAPTER 18 –

THERE WAS NO "<u>DUALITY</u> GOD" NOR A "TRINITY <u>GOD</u>" IN HEAVEN.

....

JOHN 1:1 CONTRADICTED WHAT GOD SAID IN THE OLD TESTAMENT.

Let's read John 1:1, and verse 14. (KJV).

v.1 – "IN the beginning was the Word, and the Word was <u>with</u> God, and the Word was God.

v.14 – And the Word was made flesh, and dwelt among us (and we beheld his glory, the glory as of the only begotten of the Father,) full of grace and truth."

....

JOHN ADVOCATED THE <u>DUALITY</u> GOD THEORY.

ACCORDING TO JOHN, THE GOD OF ABRAHAM + THE WORD (JESUS) WHO WAS ALSO GOD = 2 GODS.

BOTH EXISTED FROM THE BEGINNING IN HEAVEN.

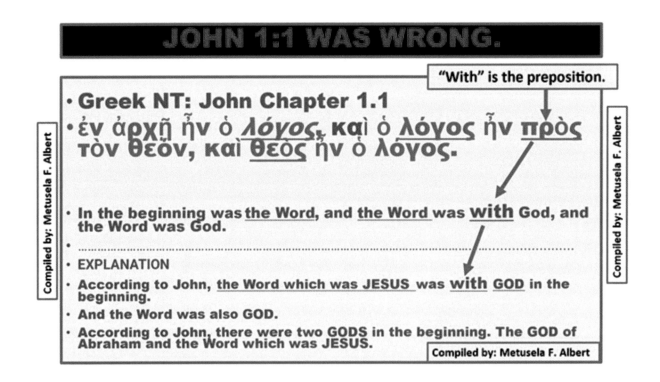

According to John,

1. The Word was JESUS who became human flesh. (Read John 1:14).

2. JESUS was <u>with</u> the Father from the beginning.

3. JESUS was also God. Read the preposition ("with") used by John in verse one.

4. The two of them existed from the beginning.

5. It was JESUS, the begotten Son of the Father who created all things, therefore, he created the angels in heaven.

6. Therefore, the Father and the Son existed in heaven before the angels were created by the Son.

7. NOTE: After Lucifer and one-third of the angels sinned in heaven, they were cast out of heaven to this planet earth. That means, they (the fallen angels) were present on earth at the time JESUS created our planet in six days and rested on the seventh day. Thus, the weekly cycle of seven days started from the Garden of Eden, at Creation time. Thus, the Sabbath existed from there, not at the time of Moses and the Israelites.

8. Adam and Eve were created on the sixth day, and the Sabbath was the seventh day. Their first complete day on earth was the Sabbath, and they were asked to observe the Seventh day as the Sabbath. The observance of the Sabbath day originated at the Garden of Eden, <u>not</u> during the wilderness Journey of the Israelites from Egypt to Canaan.

9. Therefore, JESUS created Adam and Eve on the *sixth day* before the seventh day. Read Genesis 1:27-31; Genesis 2:1-3.

10. There was <u>no</u> such thing that GOD had a begotten Son called JESUS in heaven.

11. There was no such thing that GOD the Father and a begotten Son called JESUS were Co-eternal or Co-Creators.

12. The TRUTH is: JESUS was <u>not</u> the Son of GOD in heaven because He was the only GOD in heaven.

13. Only <u>One Being</u> existed in heaven. He was JESUS.

14. There was no such thing as <u>three persons</u> existed in from eternity.

15. Because JESUS was <u>not</u> a second person in heaven, therefore, the Holy Spirit was <u>not</u> a person nor a third person.

16. The Holy Spirit was "the Spirit of GOD." It was the Spirit of JESUS since He was the only GOD – (Genesis 1:1-3).

....

Let's read John 1:1-3. (KJV).

v.1 – "In the beginning was the Word, and the Word was <u>with</u> God, and <u>the Word was God</u>.

v.2 – The <u>same</u> was in the beginning <u>with</u> God.

v.3 – All things were <u>made</u> by <u>him</u>; and without <u>him</u> was not anything made that was made."

NOTE: According to John in the New Testament, it was the Son of GOD who took human flesh, created heaven and earth.

According to John, The GOD OF ABRAHAM + The SON OF GOD = 2 GODS. This is the <u>DUALITY</u> GOD theory.

WHEN YOU KNOW THE TRUTH, YOU WILL EASILY KNOW THE ERROR.

THE TRUTH ABOUT THE CREATOR. HE WAS GOD, NOT THE SON OF GOD.	THE CONTRADICTION IN JOHN 1:1-3 and verse 14 ABOUT THE CREATOR.
• Genesis 1:1 – "In the beginning God created the heaven and the earth." • NOTE: God (Elohim) was the Creator. • Genesis 1:1 did NOT say, In the beginning the Son of God created heaven and earth. • NOTE: GOD DID NOT HAVE A SON IN HEAVEN CALLED JESUS. • THE TRUTH: GOD BECAME THE SON OF GOD THROUGH MARY AT BETHLEHEM AND WAS CALLED - JESUS.	• v 1. In the beginning was the Word, and the Word was with God, and the Word was God. • v 2. The same was in the beginning with God. • v 3. All things were made by him; and without him was not any thing made that was made. • v 14. And the Word was made flesh, and dwelt among us (and we beheld his glory, the glory as of the only begotten of the Father,) full of grace and truth. • NOTE: John advocated that the Son of God called JESUS was also God, created heaven and earth. • John also advocated the "DUALITY GOD" because of the use of the Preposition "WITH" in John 1:1.

Compiled by: Metusela F. Albert. Dated: 08/18/2024.

John <u>contradicted</u> Genesis 1:1 and Isaiah 43:10-11.

LET'S READ ISAIAH 43:10-11.

10. "Ye are my witnesses, <u>saith the LORD</u>, and my servant whom I have chosen: that ye may know and believe me, and understand that <u>I am he: before me there was no God formed, neither shall there be after me</u>.

11. I, even I, am <u>the LORD</u>; and <u>beside me there is no Saviour</u>."

LET'S READ ISAIAH 44:6, 24; 45:5 and 49:16.

Isaiah 44:6, Thus saith <u>the LORD</u> the King of Israel, and his redeemer the LORD of hosts; <u>I am the first, and I am the last; and beside me there is no God</u>.

………………………………………………………………………………………………

Isaiah 44:24, Thus saith <u>the LORD</u>, thy redeemer, and <u>he that formed thee from the womb</u>, <u>I am the LORD</u> that maketh all things; that stretcheth forth the heavens <u>alone</u>; that spreadeth abroad the earth by <u>myself</u>;

....

Isaiah 45:5, "I am <u>the LORD</u>, and there is <u>none else, there is no God beside me</u>: I girded thee, <u>thou hast not known me</u>."

....

Isaiah 49:16, "Behold, <u>I have graven thee upon the palms of my hands</u>; thy walls are continually before me."

....

EXPLANATION

NOTE: The GOD who spoke to the Prophet Isaiah was the "ELOHIM" who created heaven and earth. Isaiah 49:16 was a prophecy of the *kind* of death HE would die. It was by crucifixion. This refers to none other than JESUS.

NOTE: JESUS WAS THE GOD (ELOHIM) WHO CREATED HEAVEN AND EARTH, WHO LATER BECAME THE GOD OF ABRAHAM, ISAAC, JACOB, AND ALL THE PROPHETS.

....

NO SON OF GOD EXISTED FROM ETERNITY.

NOTE: SINCE "JESUS" WAS THE <u>ELOHIM</u> WHO CREATED HEAVEN AND EARTH, WHO BECAME THE GOD OF ABRAHAM, WHO SPOKE TO THE PROPHET ISAIAH, WE CAN NOW CONCLUDE THAT THERE WAS NO SON OF GOD CALLED JESUS THAT EXISTED BEFORE THE ANGELS EXISTED IN HEAVEN.

WE CAN ALSO CONCLUDE THAT JOHN CONTRADICTED GENESIS 1:1 AND ISAIAH 43:10-11.

....

When you know the truth, you will surely know the error. Any error is very easy to notice, once you know the truth. Since JESUS was the Elohim who created heaven and earth, therefore, John 1:1 is wrong for telling us that the Son of God created heaven and earth. Therefore, John 3:16, contradicted what God said who he was, in Genesis 1:1-3 and Isaiah 43:10-11; 44:6, 24; 49:16.

> # JESUS WAS THE "ELOHIM" WHO CREATED HEAVEN AND EARTH – Genesis 1:1, 27-31; 2:1-3.
> 1. When you read the Old Testament, you would find that there was <u>only one God; not three Gods</u>. Isaiah 43:10-11.
> 2. JESUS was the "YAHWEH" of the Prophets.
> 3. JESUS was the "JEHOVAH" of Moses – Ex. 6:1-3.
> 3. JESUS was the "I AM THAT I AM" who spoke to Moses at the burning bush. He wrote the Ten Commandments. Ex. 20:1-3.
> 4. JESUS was the "I AM THAT I AM" who spoke to John the Revelator on the Island of Patmos.
>
> Try and Read Genesis 1:1-3, 5, 10, 16, Exodus 20:1-3; John 5:39. 46; 8:56-58.
> Further reading: Isaiah 44:6,24; 49:16; Revelation 21:6-7.
>
> There is NO such thing called – God the Father, God the Son, God the Holy Spirit. . . . No such thing as 3 Gods. . . . No Trinity.
>
> Compiled by: Metusela F. Albert.

....

ANOTHER SCRIPTURE: 2 John 1:3, 9.

v.3 - Grace be with you, mercy, and peace from <u>God the Father, and from the Lord Jesus Christ, the Son of the Father</u>, in truth and in love.

v.4 – Whosoever transgresseth, and abideth not in the doctrine of Christ, hath no God. He that abideth in the doctrine of Christ, <u>he hath both the Father and the Son.</u>

....

NOTE: John repeated again in the above Scriptures (2 John 1:3, 9) that the Father and the Son of GOD were <u>TWO distinct Beings</u>.

This <u>DUALITY GOD</u> theory advocated by John, in John 1:1 and John 3:16, was reinforced in 2 John 1:1, 3, 9.

....

WHAT ABOUT WHEN JESUS WAS ON THE CROSS, AND HE SAID, "Father, forgive them; for they know not what they do." (Luke 23:34).

ISN'T THE FATHER A DISTINCT PERSON FROM JESUS?

Scripture - Luke 23:46. And when JESUS had cried with a loud voice, he said, "Father, into thy hands I commend my spirit: and having said thus <u>he</u> gave up the ghost".

....

REMEMBER THIS: JESUS had *two natures* while he was in human flesh.

Read Chapter 10 of this book about the <u>Two Natures</u> of JESUS.

As a human being, he was tortured by the Romans and died on the Cross. As God, his divine nature did not die because God cannot die. His divine nature was not tortured.

Being human, he spoke to the Father in heaven who existed in Spirit form. God is omnipotent, he can speak to us from the sky in English or in Spanish or in Greek or in German or in French or in Hindu or in whatever language. His voice can echo from heaven and the whole world can hear it despite the distance and location. Nothing is impossible for God. All things are possible for JESUS.

....

JOHN 3:16 <u>CONTRADICTED</u> WHAT GOD SAID IN THE OLD TESTAMENT.

2 John 1:3, 9 also Contradicted Isaiah 43:10-11.

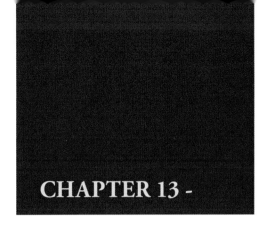

CHAPTER 13 -

PAUL CONTRADICTED WHAT GOD SAID IN THE OLD TESTAMENT.

Let's see Paul's belief about the Father and Jesus?

Read Paul's open greeting in his letters to the Churches. Take note of the greeting phrase: "Grace, mercy, and peace, from God our Father, and the Lord Jesus Christ."

Evidently, Paul <u>believed</u> that the Father and the Son of God were <u>TWO distinct beings in heaven.</u>

Paul <u>believed</u> that Jesus was *the firstborn* of the Father in heaven. In other words, Jesus was a creature with a beginning in heaven. (Colossians 1:15-18).

Paul did <u>not</u> know that Jesus was the God ("Elohim") who created heaven and earth in Genesis 1:1.

Paul did <u>not </u>know that Jesus was <u>not </u>the Son of God in heaven.

Did you notice in Colossians 1:15-18, that Paul referred to Jesus as the *firstborn* of all creatures?

BELOW YOU WOULD READ PAUL'S GREETINGS TO THE CHURCHES. HE DEFINED THE FATHER AND JESUS, AS TWO DISTINCT BEINGS.

Romans 1:7 – To all that be in Rome, beloved of God, called to be saints: Grace to you and peace <u>from God our Father, and the Lord Jesus Christ.</u>

1 Corinthians 1:3 – Grace be unto you, and peace, <u>from God our Father, and from the Lord Jesus Christ.</u>

2 Corinthians 1:2 – Grace be to you, and peace from <u>God our Father, and from the Lord Jesus Christ.</u>

Ephesians 1:2 – Grace be to you, and peace from <u>God our Father, and from the Lord Jesus Christ.</u>

Ephesians 2:3 – Blessed be <u>the God and Father of our Lord Jesus Christ,</u> who hath blessed us with all spiritual blessings in heavenly places in Christ:

Ephesians 2:4 – According as he hath choses us in him before the foundation of the world, that we should be holy and without blame before him in love.

Colossians 1:2 – Grace be unto you, and peace, <u>from our Father and the Lord Jesus Christ.</u>

Colossians 1:14. In whom we have redemption through his blood, even the forgiveness of sins:

Colossians 1:15 – Who is the image of the invisible God, <u>the firstborn</u> of every creature.

Colossians 1:16 – For by him were all things created, that are in heaven, and that are in earth, visible and invisible, whether they be thrones, or dominions, or principalities, or powers: all things were created by him, and for him.

Colossians 1:17 – And he is before all things, and by him all things consist.

1 Thessalonians 1:2 – Grace be unto you, and peace, <u>from God our Father, and the Lord Jesus Christ.</u>

2 Thessalonians 1:2 – Grace unto you, and peace, <u>from God our Father and the Lord Jesus Christ</u>.

1 Timothy 1:2 – Grace, mercy, and peace, <u>from God our Father and Jesus Christ our Lord</u>.

2 Timothy 1:2 – Grace, mercy, and peace, <u>from God our Father and Jesus Christ our Lord</u>.

Titus 1:4 – Grace, mercy, and peace, <u>from God the Father and the Lord Jesus Christ our Savior</u>.

Philemon 1:3 – Grace to you, and peace, <u>from God our Father and the Lord Jesus Christ</u>.

Hebrews 1:1 – GOD, who at sundry times and in divers manners spake in time past unto the fathers by the prophets,

Hebrews 1:2 – Hath in these last days spoken unto us <u>by his Son</u> who he hath appointed heir of all things, by whom also <u>he made the worlds</u>;

Hebrews 1:6 – And again, <u>when he bringeth in the first begotten into the world, he saith, And let all the angels of God worship him</u>.

Hebrews 1:8 – <u>But unto the Son he saith, Thy throne, O God, is for ever and ever</u>: a sceptre of righteousness is the sceptre of thy kingdom.

....

Hebrews 12:2 – Looking unto <u>Jesus</u> the author and finisher of our faith: who for the joy that was set before him endured the cross despising the shame, and <u>is set down at the right hand of the throne of God</u>.

....

EXPLANATION -

NOTE: ACCORDING TO PAUL, GOD THE FATHER AND THE SON WERE <u>TWO DISTINCT GODS</u>, SITTING ON THE THRONE. THE SON WAS ON <u>THE RIGHT HAND OF THE FATHER.</u> (Hebrews 1:6, 8; 12:2).

....

NOTE: PAUL IS ADVOCATING <u>A DUALITY</u> GOD THEORY IN HEBREWS 1:6, 8; 12:2. TWO GODS ON THE THRONE. THIS IS THE SAME THEORY BY JOHN IN JOHN 1:1.

That contradicted Revelation Chapter 4:1-11 and 21:6-7; 22:11-14).

PETER CONTRADICTED WHAT GOD SAID IN THE OLD TESTAMENT. 1 PETER 1:3.

WHO WAS THE HOLY SPIRIT? NOT A THIRD PERSON, IN HEAVEN.

CHAPTER 16

ELOHIM (YAHWEH / JEHOVAH) HAD NO BEGOTTEN SON, IN HEAVEN.

CLARIFY MATTHEW 3:16-17 AND MATTHEW 28:19-20.

LET'S READ – Matthew 3:16-17.

v16. And <u>Jesus</u> when <u>he</u> was baptized, went up straightway out of the water: and, lo, the heavens were open unto <u>him</u>, and <u>he</u> saw <u>the Spirit of God descending like a dove</u>, and lighting upon <u>him</u>:

v17. And lo <u>a voice from heaven</u>, saying, This is my beloved Son, in whom I am well pleased.

....

Let's try and understand the two verses above.

1. JESUS as a human being like us was baptized by John the Baptist in the Jordan River, at age 30.

2. JESUS was <u>the Son of God by the INCARNATION process</u> through Mary at Bethlehem - (Luke 1:35).

3. Most Jews at the time of Jesus' baptism, have never understood that He was the Son of God by INCARNATION.

4. At the Jordan River, the voice that spoke from heaven, declared JESUS to be GOD'S Son. That was to help convince the unbelieving Jews regarding JESUS as the Messiah.

5. After JESUS' baptism, He did Ministry for three and a half years till his death at Calvary, 31 A.D.

6. Had the Jewish leaders believed in JESUS as the Messiah to come, they would have not killed him; but their unbelief led them to kill him, as Prophesied in Isaiah 53:1-10.

7. The Jews believed that Joseph committed fornication with Mary and JESUS was an illegitimate child born outside of wedlock. This information veiled them from seeing the Prophecies about their unbelief and killing him.

WHO WAS THE FATHER WHO SPOKE FROM HEAVEN AT JESUS' BAPTISM?

1. Was He another distinct person from JESUS? No!

2. That was JESUS who spoke from heaven.

3. While JESUS was in the water in human flesh, his voice spoke from heaven as the Father, the GOD of Abraham.

4. JESUS was in Spirit form; his voice spoke from heaven.

5. Do you remember, when He spoke to Moses from the burning bush? – Exodus 3:1-10.

6. Do you remember, when He spoke from Mount Sinai during the giving of the Ten Commandments? Nobody saw God, but his voice was heard, warning the Israelites to stay away from touching the Mountain. Anyone who touches the Mountain will surely die – Exodus 19.

7. JESUS was the GOD of Abraham and the Prophets in the Old Testament.

8. POINT: There was _no_ such thing as a Trinity GOD. No Three Distinct Persons exist in heaven.

WHAT ABOUT THE HOLY SPIRIT THAT CAME DOWN UPON JESUS, LIKE A DOVE?

1. The Holy Spirit was _not_ a person.

2. The Holy Spirit was the Spirit of JESUS, the power of the Highest.

3. The Holy Spirit is _not_ a person. It is <u>the power of the Highest</u> which caused Mary to be pregnant with the child, JESUS. (Luke 1:35).

4. At the Baptism of JESUS, His voice spoke from heaven to affirm to the unbelieving Jews of the status of JESUS, the Son of God that was born of Mary. HE was the GOD of Abraham and the prophets in the Old Testament who came in human flesh.

....

LET'S READ – Matthew 28:18-20.

v18 – And <u>Jesus</u> came and spake unto them, saying, All power is given unto <u>me</u> in heaven and in earth.

v19 – Go ye therefore, and teach all nations, baptizing them in <u>the name of the Father, and of the Son, and of the Holy Ghost:</u>

v.20 – Teaching them to observe all things whatsoever <u>I</u> have commanded you: and, lo, <u>I</u> am with you always, even unto the end of the world. Amen.

1. JESUS who was in <u>human flesh, cannot do</u> miracles on his own.

2. JESUS who has <u>divine nature</u> while in human flesh, <u>can perform miracles by his own divine power.</u>

THERE IS ONLY ONE DIVINE PERSON, NOT THREE DISTINCT BEINGS.

Remember, JESUS was <u>the Father</u> of the children of Israel in the Old Testament who <u>took human flesh and became the Son of GOD</u> through Mary at Bethlehem. The Holy Ghost (Holy Spirit) is the power of JESUS, the Most High. The Holy Spirit is <u>not </u>a third person.

NOTE: The Trinity GOD believers failed to understand Matthew 3:16-17 and Matthew 28:18-20 because they did *not* understand what GOD (JESUS) said to Prophet Isaiah in Isaiah 43:10-11, 49:16; 9:6; 7:14.

....

Let's Read; John 14:6-9.

v6 – Jesus saith to Thomas, I am the way, the truth, and the life: no man cometh unto the Father, but by me.

v7 – If ye had known me, ye should have known my Father also: and henceforth ye know him, and have seen him.

v8 – Philip saith unto him, Lord, shew us the Father, and it sufficeth us.

v9 – Jesus saith unto him, Have I been so long time with you, and yet hast thou not know me, Philip? He that hath seen me hath seen the Father, and how sayest thou then, Shew us the Father?

v10 – Believest thou not that I am in the Father, and the Father in me? The words that I speak unto you I speak not of myself: but the Father that dwelth in me, he doeth the works.

v11 – Believe me that <u>I am in the Father, and the Father in me</u>: or else believe me for the very works' sake.

v15 – If ye love <u>me</u>, keep <u>my</u> commandments.

v16 – And <u>I will pray the Father</u>, and <u>he</u> shall give you <u>another Comforter</u>, that he may abide with you forever,

....

JOHN 15:10

v10 – Jesus said, If ye keep my commandments, ye shall abide in my love, even as I have kept my Father's commandments, and abide in his love.

CHAPTER 18

THERE WAS NO "DUALITY GOD" NOR A "TRINITY GOD" IN HEAVEN.

Most Professed Christians and Mainline Churches continue to believe in a TRINITY GOD, yet we are living in 2024, almost 2,000 years since the death and resurrection of JESUS CHRIST at Calvary, 31 A.D.

The Old Testament was so clear about the CREATOR who was _not_ a TRINITY GOD. Of course, the GOD of Noah and his family was _not_ a Trinity God. And the GOD of Abraham and the Israelites was _not_ a TRINITY GOD.

In John 5:39, JESUS said: "Search the Scriptures; for in them ye think you have eternal life; but they are they which testify of _me_."

....

At the time when JESUS spoke those words recorded in John 5:39, it was only the Old Testament that existed. The Old Testament was the <u>Scripture</u>. And the GOD that was mentioned in the 66 Books of the Old Testament was none other than JESUS, himself. . . . The GOD (ELOHIM) who communed with Adam and Eve at the Garden of Eden, later took Human Flesh through Mary at Bethlehem and was called – JESUS, the Son of GOD. He later died at Calvary to be mankind's Sin Bearer / Savior. JESUS was the Father who became the Son of GOD at Bethlehem. This is the INCARNATION miracle that most people failed to understand.

Dear folks, read the Book of Isaiah, and learn that JESUS who was born of virgin Mary was the One Prophesied to be born of a virgin woman; and his name is – "WONDERFUL, COUNSELLOR, MIGHTY GOD, EVERLASTING FATHER, PRINCE OF PEACE" - (Isaiah 9:6).

His name was also called – "EMMANUEL", meaning, "GOD WITH US". (Isaiah 7:14; Matthew 1:22-23). Unfortunately, the Pharisees and the Scribes failed to understand the Prophesy in Isaiah 49:16 and 53:1-10 that mentioned the CRUCIFIXION, the kind of death He would take to save us from sin. But the sad thing today is, most Professed Christians and mainline Denominations still have not understood it.

If JESUS were on earth today (2024), is it possible that we who professed to believe in GOD would have killed JESUS for not believing in Him as the only GOD in heaven, meaning there was no Trinity GOD in heaven? Of course. Therefore, we are worse than the Jews who killed him at Calvary, about two thousand years ago.

....

THE TRINITY GOD THEORY IS ANTI-CHRIST.

- The Trinity GOD theory promotes the idea that JESUS cannot be GOD by himself; for he must be added to another Two Divine Beings; the Father and the Holy Spirit, to make one GOD.
- They call it – "THREE IN ONE."
- 1 + 1 + 1 = 1 GOD.
- THE TRINITY GOD THEORY IS ANTI-CHRIST.

Compiled by: Metusela F. Albert.

CONCLUSION

I hope this book is of some help to your understanding of who "JESUS" was, the only "GOD" who created heaven and earth. HE was the "ELOHIM" who created heaven and earth. HE became the GOD of Abraham who later took human flesh by the _INCARNATION_ process at Bethlehem through Mary and was called - the Son of GOD.

JESUS was GOD the Father who incarnated through Mary at Bethlehem and was born as the Son of GOD. – (Luke 1:35).

The GOD of Abraham, the I AM THAT I AM, did _not_ have a Begotten Son in heaven. There was _no_ such thing as three people existed in heaven making up one GOD. The Holy Spirit was _not_ a person _nor_ a third person.

Of course, GOD did _not_ have a Son called JESUS, in heaven, because JESUS was the only GOD who existed from eternity

WHEN YOU KNOW THE TRUTH, YOU WILL EASILY KNOW THE ERROR.

THE TRUTH ABOUT THE CREATOR. HE WAS GOD, NOT THE SON OF GOD.	THE CONTRADICTION IN JOHN 1:1-3 and verse 14 ABOUT THE CREATOR.
• Genesis 1:1 – "In the beginning God created the heaven and the earth." • NOTE: God (Elohim) was the Creator. • Genesis 1:1 did NOT say, In the beginning the Son of God created heaven and earth. • NOTE: GOD DID NOT HAVE A SON IN HEAVEN CALLED JESUS. • THE TRUTH: GOD BECAME THE SON OF GOD THROUGH MARY AT BETHLEHEM AND WAS CALLED - JESUS.	• v 1. In the beginning was the Word, and the Word was with God, and the Word was God. • v 2. The same was in the beginning with God. • v 3. All things were made by him; and without him was not any thing made that was made. • v 14. And the Word was made flesh, and dwelt among us (and we beheld his glory, the glory as of the only begotten of the Father,) full of grace and truth. • NOTE: John advocated that the Son of God called JESUS was also God, created heaven and earth. • John also advocated the "DUALITY GOD" because of the use of the Preposition "WITH" in John 1:1.

Compiled by: Metusela F. Albert. Dated: 08/18/2024.

....

If you still have <u>not</u> understood who JESUS was, then please read it again.

Make sure you understand the three different views about GOD in Chapter 1.

I believe that JESUS was the only GOD in heaven. HE was the "ELOHIM" who created heaven and earth. HE humbled himself and took the <u>INCARNATION</u> process through Mary at Bethlehem and became the Son of GOD. HE who was the ELOHIM (YAHWEH / JEHOVAH) came down to our level. That is the reason GOD did <u>not</u> have a Son called JESUS from eternity before the angels were created. Not only that. What else? There was <u>NO</u> third person in heaven called HOLY SPIRIT.

In heaven, Lucifer wanted to be like <u>the most High</u>; not wanted to be like the Son of GOD because there was <u>NO</u> Son of GOD in heaven. (Isaiah 14:12-14).

Don't forget, JESUS was the GOD (ELOHIM) who created Lucifer and the angels in heaven, who later *incarnated* into human flesh through Mary at Bethlehem and became the Son of GOD called JESUS, who came to die at Calvary as the Savior. It was GOD the FATHER who became the Son of

GOD. GOD did <u>not</u> send a Son to die at Calvary because there was NO Son of GOD, in heaven.

GOD loves us because <u>HE gave [himself]</u> instead of sending a Son, to die in our behalf. If GOD had sent a Son to die for us at Calvary instead of HIMSELF, then it reveals that GOD did <u>not</u> love His Son.

....

AN ANALOGY TO PROVOKE OUR THOUGHTS -

If an intruder entered your house to rob, would you send your son to face the intruder and die, OR would you confront the intruder yourself?

In our case, GOD gave His own life to die at Calvary. GOD did <u>not</u> send a Son because HE had <u>no</u> Son. Even if HE had a Son, HE would <u>not</u> send him to die. HE had unlimited angels in heaven yet sent none to die.

HAVE YOU THOUGHT ABOUT THIS?

Since GOD created the angels in heaven, HE could easily create more than one Son without a problem. If GOD had sent a Son to die at Calvary, HE could create another Son or two more Sons, to replace the Son sent down to earth.

What would stop GOD from creating a Son or two Sons? Nothing.

REMEMBER, GOD gave <u>Himself</u> by the *Incarnation* process through Mary at Bethlehem. GOD did not send a Son because GOD did not have a begotten Son in heaven.

THE TRUTH IS:

GOD had NO begotten Son in heaven called JESUS, before the angels were created, thus HE sent NO Son to die at Calvary.

It was GOD himself who <u>incarnated</u> into human flesh through Mary at

Bethlehem and became the Son of GOD called JESUS and died at Calvary as our Sin Bearer / Savior / Redeemer.

Truly, this is the Amazing UNCONDITIONAL love of GOD.

....

GOD DID NOT HAVE A SON IN HEAVEN.

Compiled by: Metusela F. Albert.

- · THINK ABOUT THIS.
- · JOHN 3:16, SHOULD HAVE BEEN WRITTEN THIS WAY TO AVOID CONTRADICTING GENESIS 1:1 AND ISAIAH 43:10-11.
- · "For GOD so loved the world, that HE humbly condescended and _incarnated_ into human flesh through Mary at Bethlehem by His own power, and became the Son of Mary who was also called the Son of GOD. HE gave [Himself] to die at Calvary as our Savior, to give eternal life to whosoever that believeth in Him, who was the only GOD that existed from eternity."

Compiled by: Metusela F. Albert.

Before I end the Book. Let me suggest one thing for you. Please, try and get hold of one of these three books listed below, and read for further understanding of who JESUS was in the Old Testament.

You can get any of these Books from www.xlibris.com or from www.amazon.com or from www.barnessandnobles.com

THERE IS NO TRINITY GOD IN HEAVEN.

BOOK - PUBLISHED ON DECEMBER 16, 2020

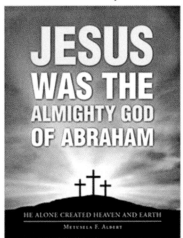

BOOK - PUBLISHED ON JANUARY 22, 2021

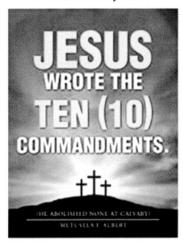

BOOK - PUBLISHED ON SEPTEMBER 12, 2021

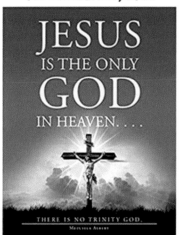

Once you come to a good understanding that JESUS was the GOD (ELOHIM) who created heaven and earth, who later became the GOD of Abraham, who later took human flesh at Bethlehem through Mary, and was called the Son of GOD, thus you will now realize that JESUS was <u>not</u> the Son of GOD from eternity.

Therefore, common sense should tell you that there was <u>NO</u> such thing as GOD had a begotten Son in heaven from eternity.

THE CASE IS <u>NOW CLOSED</u> AFTER ALL EVIDENCE WAS PROVIDED THAT <u>JESUS</u> WAS THE GOD OF THE OLD TESTAMENT PROPHETS, AND HE ALONE EXISTED FROM ETERNITY. HE WAS <u>NOT</u> A TRINITY GOD.

Therefore, GOD did <u>not</u> have a Begotten Son in heaven before the angels were created.

JESUS, WHO WAS THE GOD (ELOHIM) WHO CREATED HEAVEN AND EARTH, HUMBLY INCARNATED THROUGH MARY AT BETHLEHEM

AND WAS BORN AS THE SON OF GOD, WHO LATER DIED AT CALAVARY AS OUR SIN BEARER / SAVIOR.

THEREFORE, ALL EVIDENCE PROVED THAT GOD DID <u>NOT</u> HAVE A BEGOTTEN SON IN HEAVEN CALLED – JESUS.

THE EVIDENCE PROVIDED ALSO PROVED THAT - IN HEAVEN, THERE WAS NO PERSON CALLED HOLY SPIRIT.

FUTHERMORE, THE TEACHING OF <u>THE TRINITY GOD</u> WHICH IS <u>THE TRIUNE GOD THEORY,</u> SHOULD BE CONFRONTED AND CONDEMNED WITHOUT SPARING THE ROD.

PRAISE THE NAME OF <u>JESUS</u> AND GIVE <u>HIM</u> THE GLORY DUE TO <u>HIM</u> FOR BEING <u>OUR CREATOR WHO BECAME OUR SAVIOR AT CALVARY.</u> HE WHO WROTE THE LAW IS COMING BACK TO JUDGE US BY THE LAW.

Remember this from today,

God

did <u>not</u> have a begotten Son.

A FRIENDLY REMINDER.

JOHN 3:16, SHOULD HAVE BEEN WRITTEN THIS WAY TO AVOID CONTRADICTING GENESIS 1:1 AND ISAIAH 43:10-11 IN THE OLD TESTAMENT.

"For God so loved the world, that he humbly condescended and _incarnated_ into human flesh through Mary at Bethlehem by his own power and became the Son of Mary who was also called <u>the Son of GOD</u> who gave [himself] to die at Calvary as our Savior, <u>to give eternal life to whosoever that believeth in him as the only GOD that exists from eternity.</u>"

....

EXPLANATION: Jesus was the Son of Mary called the Son of God <u>at Bethlehem</u>. Prior to the incarnation at Bethlehem, Jesus was the ELOHIM (YAHWEH / JEHOVAH) who created heaven and earth. He <u>alone</u> existed from eternity.

Jesus was <u>*not*</u> only the Son of Mary at Bethlehem, but <u>the Son of God</u>, also. <u>Two natures</u>, the divine and the human natures, were in him. While Jesus was human, he was also divine; he did <u>*not*</u> cease from being God. He veiled his divinity while in humanity.

It was JESUS CHRIST'S *humanity* that died at Calvary, <u>not</u> his *divinity.* And it was <u>his</u> *humanity* that resurrected at Calvary. JESUS was the Father who resurrected himself because He had divine power. JESUS said in John 2:19, "Destroy this temple, and in three days <u>I</u> will raise it up."

JESUS is the resurrection and the life – (John 11:25). HE was, and is, GOD.

....

I URGE YOU TO UNDERSTAND THIS IMPORTANT POINT:

MOST PROFESSED CHRISTIANS AND THEIR DENOMINATIONS FAILED TO UNDERSTAND THESE <u>THREE REASONS</u> THAT MAKE THEM CONTINUE TO BELIEVE IN A FALSE TRINITY GOD.

Reason # 1 - They believe that everything written in the Bible is GOD'S Word, therefore, they concluded that the Bible <u>cannot</u> contradict. They quote 2 Timothy 3:16 and 1 Peter 1:20 -21.

Reason # 2 – They failed to learn that Satan's words were written in the Bible. They have made Satan's words to be equal to GOD'S words by telling us that everything in the Bible is GOD'S word.

Reason # 3 – They failed to TEST their belief about JESUS by the Old Testament. Thus, they failed to notice that John's belief about GOD (John

1:1) contradicted what GOD said who He was, in the Old Testament (Isaiah 43:10-11).

As a result, they failed to recognize the Contradiction by John, Paul, and Peter about JESUS.

....

NOTE: What the New Testament writers wrote about JESUS <u>as the Son of GOD in heaven</u>, was <u>NOT</u> correct; it contradicted what GOD said who He was, to the Prophets in the Old Testament.

....

QUESTIONNAIRE – 14 QUESTIONS TO TEST YOUR UNDERSTANDING.

1.   In heaven, Lucifer wanted to be like "the Son of God"? True or False

....

2.   If you answered, False, then explain

....

3.   Who was the God (Elohim) who created heaven and earth?

....

4.   Who was the God of Abraham?

....

5.   Who was the God who wrote the Ten Commandments on two tablets of stone at Mount Sinai?

....

6. **Who was the God who took human flesh by the incarnation process through Mary and became the Son of God at Bethlehem?**

....

7. **In heaven, there was only <u>one person</u> that existed from eternity. Who?**

....

8. **Did God NOT have a begotten Son called JESUS in heaven from eternity? Yes or No?**

....

9. **There was no DUALITY GOD in heaven. True or False?**

....

10. **There was no TRINITY GOD in heaven. True or False?**

....

11. **John 1:1 contradicted Genesis 1:1 and Isaiah 43:10-11. True or False?**

....

12. **The Son of God created heaven and earth. True OR False?**

....

Your answer for this question should <u>not</u> contradict your answer for # 3, # 7, # 8, # 10.

13. **The HOLY SPIRIT <u>is not</u> a third person in heaven. True or False?**

....

14. JESUS is the <u>First</u> and the <u>Last; the Alpha and Omega</u>. True or False?

....

THE END.

THIS IS A <u>BLANK PAGE</u> FOR <u>YOUR NOTES</u>.

Printed in the United States
by Baker & Taylor Publisher Services